GREAT BIBLE STORIES
MOSES

Adapted by Maxine Nodel   **Illustrated by Norman Nodel**

Published by Playmore Inc., Publishers, 58 Main Street, 2nd Floor, Hackensack, N.J. 07601
and Waldman Publishing Corp., 570 Seventh Avenue, New York, N.Y. 10018

BARONET BOOKS, NEW YORK, NEW YORK

Conforms to ASTM F963-96a and EN71

Printed in China

Years after Joseph died, a new Pharaoh ruled Egypt. He was cruel to the Israelites, because he feared they would become too powerful.

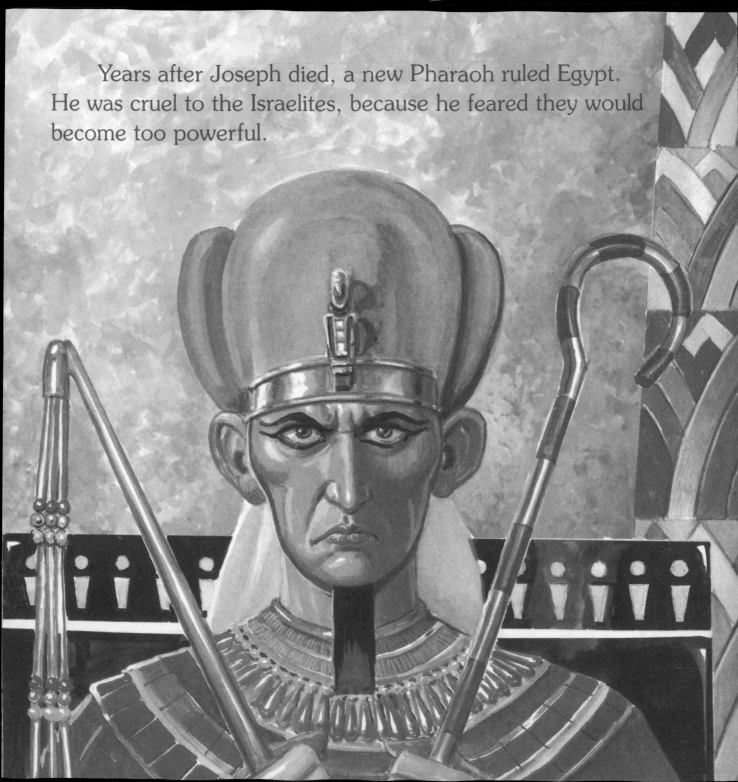

He made slaves of the Israelites who suffered under the hands of the taskmasters. Pharaoh also ordered that all newborn Hebrew baby boys be put to death.

A Hebrew mother made a basket of reeds where she hid her newborn baby boy. She floated the basket on the Nile River and told her daughter, Miriam, to watch over it.

Pharaoh's daughter was bathing at the river's edge when she noticed the basket floating in the bulrushes.

"He must be a Hebrew baby," she thought. "I will raise him and call him Moses."

Time passed and Moses saw how painfully the Hebrews lived under Pharaoh. One day, he saw an Egyptian whip a Hebrew to death. Enraged, Moses killed the Egyptian.

Moses fled to the land of Midian.

In Midian, Moses rested by a well. Suddenly, seven daughters of a priest came to the well to draw water for their sheep and goats.

Soon, shepherds came to drive them away, but Moses rescued them. The daughters brought Moses home to help them tend their flocks.

One day, Moses came upon a flaming bush. But he noticed that despite the flames, the bush wasn't really burning. Suddenly Moses heard the voice of God.

"Moses! Moses!"

"Here I am," he answered.

"I know how cruelly my people are suffering in Egypt. I shall deliver them and bring them to a rich and fertile land. Go to the king of Egypt and rescue the Israelites."

"Lord God," pleaded Moses, "please send someone else." God was not pleased with Moses for not trusting him. "Your brother, Aaron, will soon meet you. Go to Pharaoh together, and Aaron will speak for you."

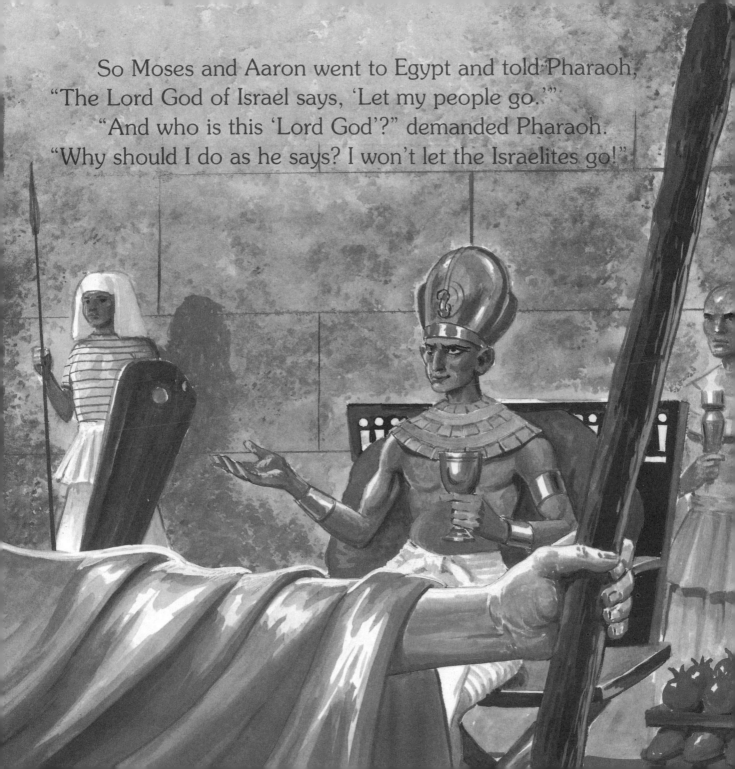

So Moses and Aaron went to Egypt and told Pharaoh,
"The Lord God of Israel says, 'Let my people go.'"
"And who is this 'Lord God'?" demanded Pharaoh.
"Why should I do as he says? I won't let the Israelites go!"

Pharaoh ordered the Egyptian slave-drivers
to stop giving the Israelites straw to make bricks.
   "Make them find the straw themselves!" he ordered.
And the slaves were beaten if they didn't make the bricks.

God told Moses to go to Pharaoh again and to warn him that terrible things would happen in Egypt if the Israelites were not freed.

"And if Pharaoh wants you to prove yourself, tell Aaron to throw down his rod and it will become a snake."

Pharaoh called over his wise men and magicians, and they magically turned their rods into snakes too. But Aaron's rod devoured theirs. Pharaoh still refused to listen to God's commands.

"Pharaoh is very stubborn," God said to Moses. "You must warn him that there will be many plagues if he does not listen. Go and meet him by the river, and take your rod. Then strike the water with it."

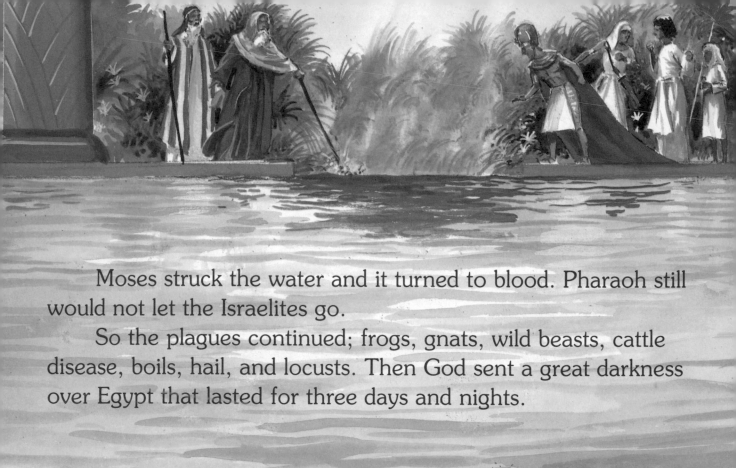

Moses struck the water and it turned to blood. Pharaoh still would not let the Israelites go.

So the plagues continued; frogs, gnats, wild beasts, cattle disease, boils, hail, and locusts. Then God sent a great darkness over Egypt that lasted for three days and nights.

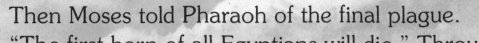

Then Moses told Pharaoh of the final plague.
"The first born of all Egyptians will die." Throughout the night there was a great cry in every Egyptian house! But the plague passed over the houses of the Hebrews.

Finally Pharaoh called for Moses and Aaron.
"Rise up and leave this land, you and all the children of Israel.
You are free to go!"

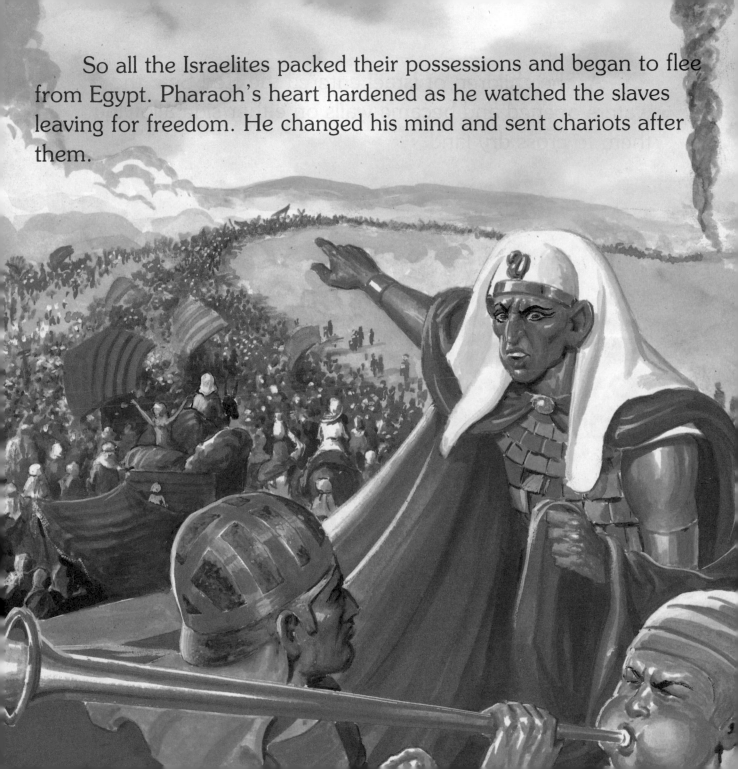

So all the Israelites packed their possessions and began to flee from Egypt. Pharaoh's heart hardened as he watched the slaves leaving for freedom. He changed his mind and sent chariots after them.

As the children of Israel entered the Red Sea, the waters opened and became walls on either side allowing them to cross dry land.

The Egyptians followed them into the midst of the sea. When the Israelites reached the other side, Moses stretched out his hand and the sea returned, swallowing up the Egyptians.

Moses led the children of Israel through the Wilderness.
On their way to Mount Sinai, God protected them, and gave them
water and a special food called manna.

Moses went up to Mount Sinai for forty days and forty nights to receive the Ten Commandments. But when he returned, he found the Israelites worshipping a golden calf! Enraged, he smashed the tablets to bits!

For a second time, Moses ascended the mountain, and when he came down, his face shone. The people of Israel accepted the Ten Commandments.

God delivered the Israelites into the promised land and blessed them.